KEEPING PETS

Freshwater Fish

Tristan Boyer Binns

Heinemann
LIBRARY

www.heinemann.co.uk/library
Visit our website to find out more information about Heinemann Library books.

To order:
☎ Phone 44 (0) 1865 888066
📄 Send a fax to 44 (0) 1865 314091
💻 Visit the Heinemann bookshop at www.heinemann.co.uk/library to browse our catalogue and order online.

First published in Great Britain by
Heinemann Library, Halley Court, Jordan Hill,
Oxford OX2 8EJ, part of Harcourt Education.

Heinemann is a registered trademark of
Harcourt Education Ltd.

Editorial: Andrew Farrow and Stig Vatland
Design: Richard Parker and Q2A Solutions
Illustrations: Jeff Edwards
Picture Research: Melissa Allison and
Virginia Stroud-Lewis
Production: Chloe Bloom

Originated by Modern Age Repro
Printed and Bound in China
by South China Printing Company

10 digit ISBN: 0 431 12426 4
13 digit ISBN: 978 0 431 12426 1

10 09 08 07 06
10 9 8 7 6 5 4 3 2 1

British Library Cataloguing in Publication Data
Binns, Tristan Boyer
Freshwater fish. - (Keeping pets)
1.Freshwater fishes - Juvenile literature
2.Aquarium fishes
639.3'4

A full catalogue record for this book is available
from the British Library.

Acknowledgements
The publishers would like to thank the following
for permission to reproduce photographs: Alamy
Images pp. **9 top** (Greenshoots Communications),
17 left middle (Maximilian Weinzierl); Ardea
pp. **7** (A. E. Bomford), 4 (Andrea Florence); Bruce
Coleman USA p. **24**; Corbis p. **15** Martin Harvey;
DK Images pp. **5**, **6 right**, **10 left**, **35**; FLPA pp. **8**
(Foto Natura Stock), **14** (Wil Meinderts/Foto
Natura); Harcourt Education Ltd (Tudor
Photography) pp. **9 inset**, **10 right**, **11**, **12**, **13**,
19 bottom, **19 top**, **20**, **21 left**, **21 right**, **23**,
25 left, **25 right**, **26**, **27**, **28 bottom**, **28 top**,
30, **31**, **32 left**, **32 right**, **34**, **36 left**, **36 right**,
37, **39 middle**, **41 bottom**, **45 bottom**, **45 top**;
Heather Angel p. **41 top** (Natural Visions);
Oxford Scientific Films p. **6 left**; PhotoEdit p. **19
bottom inset**; Photolibrary.com p. **42** (IPS Co
Ltd); Photomax pp. **17 top**, **17 bottom**, **17 right
middle**, **22**, **29 bottom**, **29 middle**, **29 top**, **33**,
38, **39 bottom**, **40**, **43**.

Cover photograph reproduced with permission of
NHPA (Joe Blossom).

Contents

Any words appearing in the text in bold, **like this**, are explained in the Glossary.

What is a freshwater fish?

Fish live in different types of water all over the world. Saltwater fish live in salt water, such as the ocean. Freshwater fish live in water that is not salty. There are many types of freshwater **environment**, such as rivers, ponds, and lakes.

This is a **habitat** for wild freshwater fish.

Different environments

All fish are **cold-blooded**. This means they cannot control their own body temperature. Their blood will be the same temperature as the water they swim in. Some fish can live in colder water than others. Some people keep pet fish outside in ponds. These fish can get very cold without dying. This book is about keeping pet fish inside in fish tanks. Some people heat their tanks, so they can keep fish from **tropical**, or warm, environments.

Different fish

Fish make great pets. They are fun to watch and interesting to learn about. Saltwater fish are harder to keep. You have to control the amount of salt in the water, and the fish are more sensitive. Most beginners start with freshwater fish.

This fish tank has been carefully designed to be like the fish's natural environment.

Need to know

- Keeping pets is a big responsibility. You must keep them healthy and look after them properly.
- If you do not look after them properly, you are making them suffer and breaking the law.
- Before you get any kind of pet, even a goldfish, make sure you will be able to care for it properly.
- You must always ask permission before you buy any pet, and you should go to the shop with an adult who can help you.

Freshwater fish facts

The best way to learn how to care for your pet fish is to learn how they live in the wild. Fish have been around for millions of years. Over time they have **adapted** to where they live. Choose fish that come from a similar **habitat**. They will need the same types of water and temperature.

Finding a level

Some fish swim near the surface of the water. Other fish swim in the middle or at the bottom. Each type has a different shaped mouth. Surface feeders have mouths that point upwards, to gather food at the top of the water. Middle feeders have mouths that point straight ahead, since their food is usually right in front of them. Bottom feeders have mouths that point downwards to suck food off the bottom.

You can see how this fish's mouth has adapted to suit where it swims. Since it lives near the surface, its mouth angles upwards to help it scoop up food easily.

In this tank, as in the wild, some of the fish swim at the top, some in the middle, and some at the bottom.

Having babies

Some fish give birth to live babies, called **fry**, but most fish lay eggs. Some eggs are attached to plants or left to float free. Others are protected in bubble nests and guarded by the parents. Some parents keep the eggs in their mouths until they are ready to hatch. Others have left by the time their babies are born. Some do not seem to know their own babies and may eat them if they are hungry!

Most fish have many babies at once. A lot of the eggs or fry may be eaten by other fish, or the young fish may not find enough food to survive. Having a lot of young is a way of making sure that some babies will survive to be adults.

This fish holds its eggs in its mouth until they hatch, then the babies swim right out!

Help with your hobby

As you get more experienced, you may want to set up and keep specialized tanks. Luckily, many experienced fish keepers like to help beginners. You can find discussion boards, clubs, and societies where experts will help you learn more about your hobby. Look on page 47 for contact information.

Parts of a fish

Freshwater fish may come in many shapes and colours, but their bodies work in the same way.

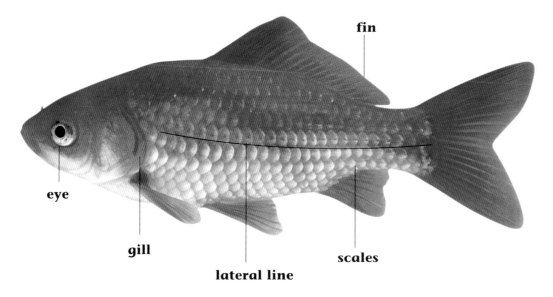

These are some of the important parts of a fish.
- The fins help the fish move. Some fins help it balance.
- Gills work like lungs to bring **oxygen** into the fish.
- The swim bladder is filled with gas. It works like a balloon to keep the fish at the right depth in the water.
- Scales cover the fish. They are like slippery, smooth plates that help it slide easily through the water.
- Nostrils help the fish smell and find food. Fish have different numbers of nostrils in different places.
- A fish's eyes are usually on either side of its head. They let the fish see almost the whole way around it.
- The lateral line is a line of pits that run along a fish's sides. Water fills the pits. As vibrations move through the water, the fish senses them. The lateral line lets the fish sense what is going on all around it.
- The skin of a fish can sense small changes in water temperature. The skin can also feel things that touch it.
- Most fish have **taste buds** in unusual places – on their heads, lips, lining their mouths, on their barbels (like whiskers). Some fish even have taste buds on their fins!

These fish are being farmed in Malaysia. They will be sent all over the world for people to enjoy in their fish tanks and ponds.

Did you know?

Collecting and breeding fish for pets is big business. But in some countries, collecting or breeding fish is harming the **environment**. There are laws to keep animals and their wild **habitats** protected. There is a special award that an international group called the Marine Aquarium Council gives to people who collect or breed fish safely.

Many fish travel a long way before they reach the tanks in a pet shop.

Are fish for you?

Fish live in water, not air. Their lives are very different from ours. This makes them interesting to watch as they swim and eat. You can learn about their natural **habitats**, how their bodies work, and what keeps them healthy.

Some people start with a couple of goldfish and become experts as they set up more and more challenging tanks. Who knows, you may become an expert yourself!

The whole family can enjoy watching your pets and learning about their lives.

Ask an adult to help you set up a new tank. You can learn about fish and their **environments** together.

Yes or no?

You need to think about the responsibility that you are taking on before you decide to keep fish. If you do not look after your fish well, they will die. Fish get **stressed** easily. Big changes in temperature, loud noises, and things banging the tank can hurt them. Your whole family has to agree where the tank will go, and understand how to keep your fish calm and happy.

Freshwater fish good points

- It is interesting to watch and learn about them.
- They can live for a long time.
- Once you get into a routine, caring for them is not difficult.
- Fish are quiet pets.
- If you or people in your family are **allergic** to fur or feathers, fish are excellent pets!

Freshwater fish not-so-good points

- Setting up a tank and buying fish can be expensive.
- Fish can get illnesses that can be hard to treat.
- If fish get ill, they need to be **isolated** in a hospital tank.
- Fish do not get to know you and are not cuddly the way other pets are.
- Sometimes fish will **breed**. This can be great, unless you get too many fish! Ask your local fish store for advice.

Caring for fish also means cleaning up after them!

Choosing a tank and fish

Congratulations on deciding to keep fish! Now you need to decide if you will heat the water in your tank so you can keep **tropical** fish. Otherwise you could keep goldfish, which are coldwater fish and do not need a heater.

Setting up your tank

Your fish tank needs to be somewhere light, but not in direct sunlight. It should not be close to a radiator or other source of heat. It should be in a room that stays about the same temperature day and night, all year. Fish like peace and quiet, so a busy hallway would not be a good choice. You also need electricity sockets nearby.

Fish need **oxygen** to breathe. Oxygen gets into the water where the water touches the air in the room. The best fish tanks are not very deep, with a wide, long top opening where the water meets the air. This means plenty of oxygen can reach your fish.

Tanks come in many shapes and sizes. You should be able to find a tank to fit the space you have at home.

On a shelf?

Most fish tanks are too big and heavy to sit on a shelf. You might need a stand for your tank. You will also need somewhere to store all the food, spare parts, nets, and other things your fish will need. A tank stand with a cupboard underneath may be a good choice.

When you buy fish, the dealer puts them in a clear plastic bag inside a paper bag. If it is very hot or cold outside, put the bag inside a **cool box**.

Top tips

- Try to get your fish somewhere local, so the water will not be very different. Very different water can make fish **stressed**.
- The shorter the journey home, the less stressed the fish will get on the way.
- Ask local experts and friends which dealer they buy from. Visit the fish supply shop and check that the fish look healthy, the water looks clear, and the staff are happy to answer your questions.

Choosing fish

Now that you have sorted out your tank, you can choose your fish. You need to work out how many fish will live happily in your tank. First, find out how many litres of water your tank holds. You then decide how many fish you can have by their length when they are fully grown. For each litre (1/4 gallon) of water, you can have about 6 mm (1/6 inch) of fish length. So in a 60 litre (15 gallon) tank, you will have enough room for about 360 mm (14 inches) of fish. A 60 litre (15 gallon) tank is about 60 x 30 x 30 cm (24 x 12 x 12 inches) big.

Special needs

Each type of fish needs certain things to keep it healthy. It may like to swim at the top, middle, or bottom of the tank. It may like very still water or moving water. It may want to be the only one of its type in your tank, have one friend, or swim in a **school** of six or more. It may want to eat other, smaller fish! Make sure you know exactly what each fish is like and what it needs.

Goldfish are great pets. Standard goldfish, like this one, can live a long time and grow very big.

Healthy fish

A healthy fish should swim with its fins out and body the right way up. It should be in the part of the tank it usually likes. It should be interested in food. There should be no spots or fuzzy **fungus** on its body. None of the fins should be torn or ragged. Finally, it should have clear eyes that do not bulge out.

Fancy goldfish can be very interesting to watch! They often have larger bodies and longer fins than common goldfish.

Setting up

At first, it is best to plan on keeping inexpensive, common fish. As you get more experienced, you can keep more unusual types. If you have a heated **tropical** tank, you can choose many different types of fish. Make a final list, but do not buy any fish yet!

Spend time looking through books and visit your fish supply shop, and see what you like. Ask what other fish live happily with the fish you like, and how many you should plan to buy. Make sure the fish you like eat food you can get easily. Make sure you choose fish that swim in all the different levels of the tank.

Settling the tank

You will need to set up the tank and let it settle for about a week before you add any fish. When it has settled, you can add one or two hardy fish. Then you must wait for the water to balance before adding any more (see page 24).

Tropical tank set-up

If you have a 60-litre (15 gallon) tank and keep the temperature between 22 and 26°C (72 to 79°F), you could keep the following group of fish. Add the tetras last, since they are the fussiest about the water.

- Six Neon Tetras – these swim in a group, called a **school**, in the middle of the tank.
- Six Penguin Tetras – these are also called Hockey Sticks, since their stripe looks like a hockey stick. They swim in a school in the middle of the tank.
- Two Dwarf Gourami – they swim in the top to middle of the tank.
- Two Corydoras – they eat food from the bottom.
- Two Swordtails – they swim in the top to middle of the tank.

Another tank setup

This group of fish would live happily in a tank together, kept between 22 and 24°C (72 to 75°F).

This is a Corydoras gossei. It is fine to keep just one. They swim at the bottom.

This is the Lace or Pearl Gourami. You will need two of them. They swim in the middle to upper level.

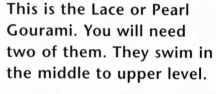

This is a Fancy Guppy. They like to live in pairs. They swim at the middle level.

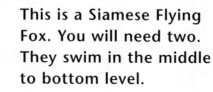

This is a Siamese Flying Fox. You will need two. They swim in the middle to bottom level.

What do I need?

To set up a new **aquarium**, you need a lot of things. Before you buy anything, decide which fish you want. Then draw up a tank plan. Since you will have already decided where the tank will go in your home, you can draw its shape and size. Find out what types of plants and hiding places the fish you have chosen need to stay happy. Wood, rocks, and clay flowerpots will look good in your tank. Add your choices to your tank plan.

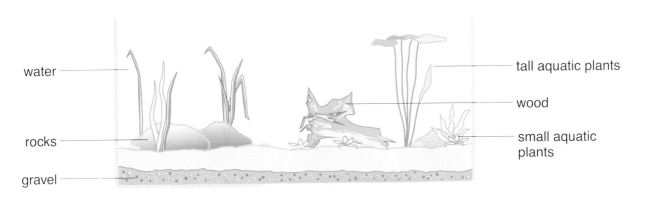

water

rocks

gravel

tall aquatic plants

wood

small aquatic plants

Before you buy anything, make sure you are happy with your tank plan.

Plug it in

Next, decide on the **filter**, heater, and **hood**. Most beginners use a simple internal sponge filter that is easy to keep clean. Some people prefer an external filter. This hangs outside the tank and sends filtered water back into the tank through a tube. Talk to your fish dealer about what is best for you. To get enough **oxygen** into the tank, many people use an **air rock** as well. These send up a stream of air bubbles that are nice to look at. Some shops sell plastic toys, such as treasure chests, that make bubbles.

If you are setting up a **tropical** tank, you need a heater as well. All tanks need a hood to protect the top and hold the light in place. Most tanks can be bought with a hood and light that fits them perfectly.

Top tip

You need to be very careful with all the electric parts of your tank. Never touch the plugs when your hands are wet. Always get an adult to handle the plugs for you.

The filter, heater, and air rock help keep your fish healthy by keeping their water just right.

Some tanks can sit on shelves, but most will need stands. Put a sheet of polystyrene under the tank. This stops the glass from breaking by spreading out the pressure on it.

At the bottom

You need to pick a **substrate**. This is the material that goes on the bottom of the tank. Medium to fine sand or gravel is best. It should be smooth, so your fish do not get hurt on it. Do not pick very coarse gravel. Dirt falls between the gaps and it is very hard to clean out. Darker colours will look the most natural.

Most people also get a background. It helps the fish to feel at home, and also looks nice. Most people stick a printed sheet on the outside of the tank. You can find moulded backgrounds that you glue to the inside of the tank before you add the water, but these can be hard to keep clean.

Choose your substrate, background, and decorations to make your fish feel at home. They also make the tank more interesting to look at.

Clean water

Even the best **filter** cannot keep the water completely clean. You need to replace some of the water every two weeks or so. Before you add new water, you should treat it with a **water conditioner**. It is a good idea to get a water testing kit. You might also like to get some chemicals for correcting the water if you ever need to. Ask your dealer what is best for the tap water where you live. You will need a tool called a siphon to move water in and out of the tank. The best ones have a bulb you squeeze to get the water moving.

Extras

You will need a few other things when you are ready to start. You will need one or two fine mesh green nets to catch your fish. An **algae** scraper is used to clean algae off the sides of the tank. Your fish depend on the filter, heater, and light to keep them healthy, so keep some spare parts in case anything breaks. Many people also have a hospital tank, to put sick fish in. A hospital tank can be a small plastic tank with a small filter and heater.

Top tip

Your **aquarium** will be home for your fish, so it needs to provide a safe and healthy **environment** for them. The aquarium also needs to be something you like looking at. Make sure your tank plan meets all of these needs.

The chemicals, siphon and algae scraper all help keep the tank water clean.

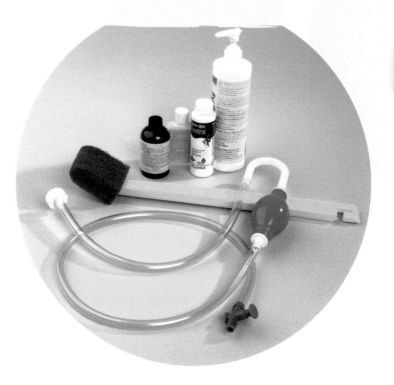

All tanks need a thermometer to tell you the water temperature. You can choose ones which go on the inside or outside of the tank.

Getting the water right

The water in your **aquarium** must be just right for your fish to live in. The fish you choose should all like the same type of water.

This aquarium is in perfect balance. The water is just right for the fish and plants that live in it.

Temperature and pH

The temperature needs to be within a range that is not too hot or too cold for your fish. The water must not be too **acidic** or **alkaline** for your fish. You measure this using a simple test called a "**pH** test". You take a small amount of the water and add a drop of testing liquid to it. The sample will change colour. You then compare the colour to a chart and it will tell you the pH of the sample. If it is too acidic or alkaline, you can use a treatment kit to correct it. After you treat it, you will need to test another sample to make sure it is right.

Hardness

Water can be "hard" or "soft". Water **hardness** refers to how many minerals are dissolved in the water. Some fish like hard water and others like soft water. You can test water hardness in the same way as you test for pH, using a special kit. You can treat it in the same way too.

Tap water contains chemicals that are bad for all fish. One, called **chlorine**, is a gas which usually goes into the air over a couple of days. But to be sure, it is still a good idea to treat your tap water for it. Others, such as **fluoride**, always need treatments to get rid of them. Ask your fish supply shop what your tap water will need to be treated for.

Top tip
Your tap water may have other chemicals in it that are bad for fish. They may be impossible to get out. You may need to use special water without any minerals to keep your fish in. Ask your pet store for advice.

Testing kits are easy to use and do not cost much. Ask your fish supply shop how often to use the ones they recommend. There are special kits for new tanks.

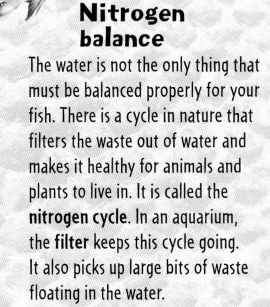

Nitrogen balance

The water is not the only thing that must be balanced properly for your fish. There is a cycle in nature that filters the waste out of water and makes it healthy for animals and plants to live in. It is called the **nitrogen cycle**. In an aquarium, the **filter** keeps this cycle going. It also picks up large bits of waste floating in the water.

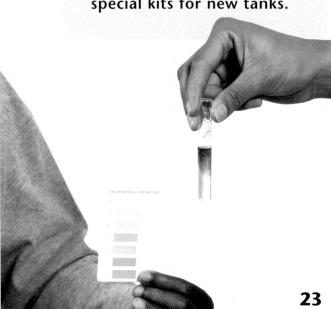

The nitrogen cycle

The **nitrogen cycle** is a process that will happen in your tank. The cycle starts when **bacteria** break down the waste that fish make. The waste turns into harmful **ammonia**. Then more bacteria turn the ammonia into **nitrites**, which are also harmful. Finally, another kind of bacteria turns the nitrites into **nitrates**, which are harmless. Nitrates even feed live plants. Live plants help the cycle work well, but they are not necessary. Over time, even with plants eating some of the nitrates, the nitrates build up in the tank water. When you change some of the water every two weeks, enough nitrates are removed to keep the water healthy.

The nitrogen cycle keeps all the food and waste in the water in balance.

Filters and bacteria

In order for this cycle to work, the sponge in the **filter** needs to have a good **colony** of the right bacteria. It takes about 36 days for the cycle to get working in a new set-up. You can shorten this time by adding gravel from an existing tank, since it will already have the right bacteria in it. You can also get treatment drops to add the bacteria to your new filter. When you clean out your filter, just swish out the solid waste in a bucket of tank water. You do not want to rinse out the bacteria colony you worked so hard to get going!

Keep it going

For the cycle to keep working well, you need to make sure there is enough **oxygen** in the water. Fish also need oxygen to breathe. Oxygen is given off in small amounts by live plants. Most of it comes from the air above the tank. **Air rocks** (see page 18) help move the water, making ripples that let more oxygen enter the tank.

Balance

- A healthy **aquarium** is in balance. It will be the best place for your fish to live.
- When an aquarium is out of balance, the water may smell or go cloudy. The fish or plants may get sick or even die.
- If the water seems off balance but your tests are all coming out fine, talk with your fish supply shop for more ideas.

You can see that this tank is out of balance! But often you cannot see that there is a problem because dangerous chemicals, such as ammonia and nitrites, are invisible.

Air rocks are easy, pretty ways to get more oxygen into the tank.

Setting up your tank

Now you are ready to set up your new **aquarium**. Before you begin, make sure you have an adult to help with the heavy lifting. Water may be clear and look light, but it weighs a great deal!

Work safely

You must also have an adult to help you with electrical items. Water and electricity do not mix. Even though all electrical items made for use with fish are safe around water, the plug and wall socket must be well away from water. When you plan how the cables and plugs will reach the sockets, make sure no-one can trip over them. Make sure the cables are safely and neatly tidied out of the way.

Planning ahead

Remember to plan ahead! Leave about a week between setting up the tank and adding one or two hardy fish. The **ammonia** from these fish will start the **nitrogen cycle**. You can also buy some products that speed up the cycle, but it usually takes about a month, and must be complete before you add any sensitive fish.

Step-by-step

1. Wash out the new tank, but never use any soap on anything for fish. Mix a little salt into tap water and use that to wash with. Rinse the salty water off with tap water.

2. Set the stand up where it will be staying. Put a polystyrene sheet on the stand (see page 19). Put the tank on the polystyrene.
3. Glue the background onto the outside of the tank and give it time to dry. A background helps fish to feel safe, since it gives them somewhere to hide.
4. Wash the **substrate** in running water until it is clear of any dirt. When you put it into the tank, rake it up so the back is higher than the front.

Top tip

Did you know that fish, like most living creatures, need day and night to stay healthy? Most like twelve hours of light and twelve hours of darkness. You may need a timer on your tank's light so it switches on and off automatically.

Getting ready for water

1. Read the instructions for your **filter**. Put the pipes and filter box in their places. Connect them all up.

2. If you are using a heater, read the instructions for it. Put the heater in the correct place. Also, place your thermometer where the instructions say it will work best. Make sure you can read the thermometer easily!

3. Wash any tank decorations in hot tap water. Some may need to be pushed firmly into your **substrate**. Add any plastic plants. Set up the decorations as you planned in your tank plan.

4. Now you can add the water. You can use water straight from the tap, but make sure it hits a rock or something large as it falls into the tank. If it goes straight onto the substrate it will make a hole in it.

There are many types of filter. Ask your local fish store which one they recommend for your tank.

5. When the tank is about two-thirds full, stop filling it. Test the water and treat it using a treatment kit.

6. Ask an adult to plug in and switch on the filter and heater. Let them run until the water is clear and up to temperature. This could take a few days. If there are any problems with the filter or heater, you can get them fixed before you put any fish in the tank.

Ask an adult to help you set up your tank.

Planting

There are many live plants you can choose for your **aquarium**. Some come with roots, to plant into the substrate. Some float on the surface of the water. Some come as **cuttings**, which then grow their own roots over time. Ask your dealer which ones will be best for your fish. Live plants help the water cycle and feed some fish. But they can be very hard to keep alive, so do not feel too bad if yours do not do well. Try different types, or switch to plastic plants.

Java Fern

Green Cabomba

Java Moss

Some plants are easier to keep than others. Ask your fish store for advice.

29

Adding plants

When the water is clearer and has reached the temperature it should be, you can add your plants.

1. Look at your tank plan as you work. Start at the back with the tallest plants and plant them in the **substrate**.
2. Finish with the shortest plants at the front and the floating ones in the water.
3. When you are happy with the planting, top up the water with tap water. Pour gently, so your planting is not ruined.
4. Fit the **hood** to the tank. Follow the instructions carefully. Ask an adult to plug in the light and set the light's on-off timer if you are using one. Always unplug the light before you take the hood off.
5. Turn on the **filter**, heater, and light. If you see any big bits of rubbish or dead plant material, take them out.

Adding fish

After a few more days, add a few hardy fish to start the **nitrogen cycle**. Ask your pet shop which fish are good. Test your water regularly, and when the cycle is complete, you can add more fish. Add one type of fish at a time, and leave about a week between each type.
It may feel like it is taking
a long time, but it will be fun
to watch as your **aquarium**
changes and grows.

If you do not put the tall plants at the back and the short plants at the front, you may never see your fish!

Water temperature

When you get your fish home from the dealer, do not open the bag straight into your tank. The new fish need to get used to the water temperature first. Float the clear plastic bag in your tank without opening it up. After about 30 minutes, you can let the fish swim out into their new home. Some experts say you should not let the water from the bag get into your tank. This is hard to do without hurting the fish. Try to get as little water as possible into your tank, but do not worry too much.

After floating the bag for about 20 minutes, add some tank water to the bag. Wait for five minutes and repeat. Then let your fish swim into their new home.

Feeding your fish

When you are planning your tank, talk to your fish dealer to make sure the fish you choose will be easy to feed. Some fish are fussy, or it is difficult to get the right type of food for them. Most fish that are good for beginners will eat dry food. Dry food is the most common kind of fish food. It comes as flakes, tablets, or pellets you buy from a fish supply shop. The flakes float on the top and feed the surface- and middle-swimming fish. Tablets sink to the bottom and feed the bottom-swimming fish.

Dry fish food comes in different forms. It has most of what fish need to eat in it.

daphnia

bloodworm

tubifex

brine shrimp

Live and frozen food

All fish like a little variety in their diet. About once a week,

Live and frozen foods give fish variety, fibre, and different **nutrients**.

it is good to feed something different. They will welcome live and frozen foods. Brine shrimp, daphnia, tubifex, and bloodworms are good options. All of these are tiny animals that fish eat in the wild. You can add lettuce leaves pushed into the **substrate** and fresh or frozen peas squashed slightly as treats for your fish as well. Take the lettuce and peas out if they are not eaten after a few hours.

When to feed?

Many experts recommend that you feed your fish dry food every other day to start with. It is important that no wasted food is left to **pollute** the water. Your fish should eat all their food in about two minutes. If they do, you can try feeding more often. Some fish need feeding twice a day, others are fine once every two days. Experiment until you get the right amount for your fish. When you have a routine, make sure you stick to it. Fish like a regular schedule. Different feeding times each day will make them **stressed**.

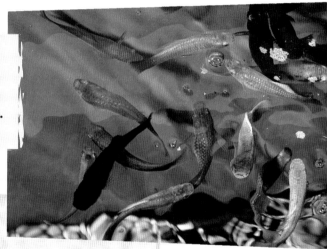

Your fish should eat in a hurry and finish all their food in about two minutes.

Are you feeding your fish too much?

- If there is food left over after two minutes, you need to clean it out. Give less food next time. Leaving food in the tank will make the water unhealthy. There may be fuzz or clumps of old food left on the bottom, too.
- If your fish are getting fat, they are eating too much. Some fish grow quickly, but they should grow evenly. If their stomachs are swelling but the rest is staying the same size, they could be overfed. If only one fish looks this way, it could be pregnant. If you are not sure, ask your fish dealer.

Keeping the tank clean

Keeping a healthy tank is the best way to keep healthy fish. The **aquarium** is much more crowded than a natural wild **habitat**. It needs your care to keep it healthy and in balance.

Every day
- Check the fish are healthy.
- Check that the water temperature is correct.
- Check that all the equipment is working.
- Feed your fish (some fish need feeding every two days).

Every week
- Clean the **hood** – but make sure you get an adult to unplug it first.
- Top up the water in your tank. Use tap water you have treated already. Remember to add the new water gently.
- Clean **algae** off the sides of the tank with a scraper.

When you clean off the algae, make sure you leave a little for the fish that like to eat it.

Every three weeks

- Stir the top of the **substrate** and siphon out any dirt.
- Do a partial water change.
- Check plants, remove any dead leaves, and trim them back if you need to. Some plants grow very quickly and can try to take over.
- Use your testing kit to check the water **pH**, **hardness**, and anything else your dealer recommends. Use your treatment kit if you need to correct anything.
- Check the **filter** sponge or material. If it is full of solid waste, take it out and wash it in the bucket of old tank water. Do not rinse it under a running tap because this will wash away the good **bacteria colony**.

Water changes

- To do a water change, prepare new water first. Treat the tap water and leave it for a few days in a bucket.
- Make sure the new water is close to the tank water temperature. Add a little hot water if you need to raise the temperature. Water that is too cold will **stress** your fish and plants.
- Use a siphon to clean the substrate as you remove the water. Take out about a tenth of the water. Do not take out any fish! Add the new water gently.

To siphon out old water, put a bucket below the tank level. Start the siphon and remove dirt from the substrate as well as water.

35

Every two months

- Change the **filter** material if needed. Never change all of it since that would take out the whole **bacteria colony**.
- Check the filter, heater, and other equipment. Ask an adult if you need to service the equipment or replace any parts. Your fish depend on the filter and heater to keep their tank healthy. If they stop working for more than a few hours, it could be serious. You should always have spare parts ready.
- Clean the filter pipework using hot water.
  Do not use any kind of soap.

Every six months

- Check the lighting tubes and get an adult to replace them if needed. You should have spare lighting tubes in case one burns out unexpectedly.

Cleaning the filter can be messy, but it is a very important job.

Set aside a special pair of scissors to use for trimming your **aquarium** plants.

Changing the lighting
tubes can be difficult.
Ask an adult to do this
for you.

Safety first

Always remember that water
and electricity do not mix.

- Never put your hands in
  the tank water when any
  of the equipment is
  plugged in.
- Ask an adult to make
  the tank safe by
  unplugging the filter,
  heater, and light.

Top tip

Looking after the everyday needs of your fish is fairly
easy. But the weekly and monthly things can be harder
to remember.

- Try making a list or chart to tell you what needs to be
  done and when.
- Or you could mark a calendar if that works better for
  you. Leave your reminder list near the tank, so you can
  see it easily.

Common problems

The water in your tank always has tiny **bacteria**, **fungus**, and **parasites** in it. Healthy fish are not affected by these things. But if the tank gets out of balance, the fish get weak and they can take over. Keeping the tank healthy is the best way to keep the fish healthy, too.

A healthy aquarium

Even the most careful fish owner will sometimes have problems. You can keep spare parts for your **filter**, heater, and lighting so they can be fixed quickly. What if your house suffers a

Fin rot makes fish look ragged. It is caused by bacteria.

power cut? First, do not panic. Most power cuts are over fairly quickly. If yours goes on for over a day, there are some things you can do. Every day, change about a tenth of the tank's water. Check the temperature, and if possible, add heated water if the temperature has fallen. Do not overfeed!

Other problems

- If your **aquarium** starts to leak, you may be able to seal it up with silicone (waterproof sticky goo) from the fish supply shop. Ask your local dealer for advice.
- Tell family and visitors not to tap the tank. Tapping the glass sounds very loud to the fish and makes them **stressed**.
- Do not put plants you find in rivers or ponds into your tank. They may have parasites living in them which could unbalance the tank. If you see a snail living in your tank, take it to the fish shop and ask what you should do.

A sick fish?

Watching your fish will help you learn their usual behaviour. Look out for fish that are behaving in a new way. Hanging near the surface or bottom, staying very still, or holding their fins in can mean a fish is ill. Some diseases are easy to see, such as if the fish is covered in spots, fluff, or worms.

Top tip

To catch a fish, gently put one net into the water. Use another net to guide the fish into the first net. Always move slowly. When you have finished with your nets, clean them in warm water or in a special chemical you can buy from the fish supply shop.

This fluffy stuff is a fungus that has grown where the fish's body was hurt.

Green nets are a good idea. Fish may think they are plants and swim into them for safety.

Hospital tank

It is a good idea to have a hospital tank set up in case one of your fish gets seriously ill. It does not need much in it. To keep it healthy, it needs a little **substrate** and a smaller **filter** and heater than your main tank. Adding a few plastic plants will help make the fish feel safe. If you have to move a sick fish to the hospital tank, keep an eye on your other fish in the main tank in case they become ill, too.

If your fish is really sick, it may need to be kept alone in a hospital tank.

Treatments

To treat most illnesses, you add medicine to the water in the tank. It is very important that you treat the water for as long as it says on the medicine packet. Even if the fish look well again sooner, finish the treatment or your fish will get infected again. Stick with one treatment until its full cycle is over. If it has not worked, then try a new one. Switching treatments too soon can make the fish get sicker.

There are not many vets who treat fish, so it is a good idea to ask an expert from a fish supply shop or fish club about puzzling illnesses. Most treatments are for the water in your tank. You get them from fish supply shops.

Common diseases

- **Fungus** – this looks like cotton wool stuck on the fish (see picture on page 39). You can treat it with a salt bath (see Top Tip) or medicine that goes in the tank water.
- Fin rot – fin rot gives a fish ragged or rotted fins (see page 38). Again, try a salt bath or medicine in the tank water.
- White spot or Ich – white spots that look like grains of sugar appear on the fish's body. It is caused by **parasites** and is treated by adding medicine from the fish supply shop to the tank water.

White spot, or Ich, spreads very quickly through the whole tank. Treat the main tank water.

Top tip

- To make a salt bath for sick fish, use a clean bowl or very small tank. Add a teaspoon of **aquarium** salt to each litre (quart) of water.
- Put the fish in the bath for about 15 minutes, but take it out if the fish seems unhappy. You might need to use less salt.
- Use a salt bath once a day until the disease has gone. Some fish are very sensitive to salt, so ask an expert before you treat a fish.

A salt bath may cure fungus or fin rot.

Parasites

Parasites are small creatures, such as worms or mites, that live on or in another creature. They can cause all sorts of problems. As well as white spot, different parasites can cause swollen eyes and holes in fish's heads. Slimy or velvety patches on the fish are signs of parasites. Parasite worms inside and outside the fish's body are also problems. If your fish have any of these problems, talk to an expert. Treatment depends on what kind of parasite it is and how sick the fish is.

A bowl is not a good home for fish! There is not enough oxygen and it is too small.

Other problems

Fish can become starved of **oxygen** if there is not enough getting into their water. They will stay gasping at the surface to try and get more. Do a partial water change as an emergency measure. Then think of how to get more oxygen into the water. An **air rock** can help by moving the water.

All aquariums have some **algae**, and some fish like to eat it. Too much may mean your tank is out of balance. Check the water **pH** and **hardness**, correct it, and clean off the algae. If the water is fine, maybe the light is on for too long each day.

Fish can get constipated, which means their **digestive systems** are not working well. They cannot push their food through properly. If any of your fish have very bloated stomachs or **faeces** hanging from their vents, they are constipated. Feed them more green vegetables such as lettuce and peas (see page 32). Also, try giving them live or frozen food such as brine shrimp.

This tank has far too much algae. It needs to be cleaned and the water needs to be tested.

Saying goodbye

Different fish live for different lengths of time. Even with the best care, some of your pet fish will die of old age or disease.

- If you find one floating in the **aquarium**, take it out with a net. It may be a shock to you, but do not blame yourself. There was probably nothing else you could have done to help it live longer.
- It is normal to feel upset when a pet dies. It may help you to have a special burial place for your fish.

Keeping a record

It is fun to watch your fish in their **aquarium**. Keeping a scrapbook lets you record that fun and remember it later. You can make notes about your fish's routines, what they eat, and how you care for them.

Even before you start setting up your tank, use a scrapbook to write down what you are learning. As you choose what to put in your tank, draw your tank plan in your scrapbook. Make notes about what choices you have made and why you have made them. If there are different ways to set up your tank, such as other plants or fish you could try, make notes about that, too. You may need to make changes later on, and your notes could help you to try new ideas.

Whenever you add new fish or plants, write about the ways you handled the changes. How did the new creatures like their home? What would you try differently next time?

Notes and photos

It is a good idea to include photos in your scrapbook. Show the tank at all stages of setting it up. As you add fish, take new pictures. You can write about why you chose those fish, and how you felt when you brought them home. If you visit a big aquarium, write about what you saw.

Your notes can help when things go wrong. If any of your fish get ill, take pictures and make notes about what you saw and did. If you need to ask an expert for advice, or if a similar problem happens again, your scrapbook will help you remember the details. Keep the numbers for your fish dealer and vet, if you have one, in your scrapbook.

After you put photos in your scrapbook, make sure you add labels to say what they show!

Top tip

Fish-keepers' clubs are good places to talk about problems and successes. Ask at your school and at your fish dealer if they know of any. If not, you could start your own. You can also ask an adult to help you find a discussion board on the Internet if you need advice. Many pet shop sites or sites about special types of fish have discussion boards.

These children meet once a month to talk about the fish they keep.

Glossary

acidic sour kind of liquid

adapted changed to suit a new environment

air rock small rock with holes connected to a pump. Sends air bubbles into the water

algae tiny water plants that grow together to make a furry coating

alkaline liquid made of special salts mixed into water

allergic when a person or an animal reacts badly to something they eat, breathe, or are stung by

ammonia a chemical that is given off when plants and animals break down after they have died

aquarium tank usually made of glass or plastic with see-through sides

bacteria tiny one-celled creatures that can cause disease or help in breaking down plant or animal matter

breed when animals mate to have babies

chlorine a chemical found in most tap water, and swimming pool water

cold-blooded animal having the same body temperature as the surrounding air or water

colony group of creatures that live together

cool box special container that keeps the temperature even inside

cuttings bits of plants that can grow into new plants

digestive system part of the body that changes food to energy and waste

environment the kind of place something lives in, with its plants, animals, weather, temperature, and landscape

faeces solid waste passed out of the body

filter machine that helps to keep the water clean

fluoride a chemical commonly added to water to help people's teeth stay strong

fry baby fish that are born live instead of in eggs

fungus a type of living thing such as mushrooms and mould

habitat the environment where a plant or animal naturally lives

hardness the measure of how many minerals are dissolved in water

hood top that covers the tank

isolated kept on its own

nitrates the end product of the nitrogen cycle – nitrates are generally harmless chemicals that are used as food by plants

nitrites chemicals made as the nitrogen cycle goes along. Nitrites are dangerous to fish and need to be turned into nitrates

nitrogen cycle the cycle that turns waste products from plants and animals into food for plants

nutrients the things in food that animals and plants need to stay healthy

oxygen a gas in air and water that animals need to breathe in order to live

parasites small creatures, such as worms or mites, that live on or in another creature

pH measure of how acidic or alkaline a liquid is

pollute to make dirty with rubbish or chemicals

school a group of fish that swim together

stressed made unhappy

substrate the material put on the bottom of an aquarium

taste buds things that people and animals use to taste their food

tropical tropical fish live in water that is quite warm in areas near the equator

water conditioner a special liquid that takes chlorine out of tap water

Further reading

Care for Your Tropical Fish, RSPCA Pet Guides Series (Collins, 2005)

Looking After Your Goldfish, Helen Piers (Frances Lincoln, 2002)

The Wild Side of Pet Fish, Jo Waters (Raintree, 2005)

Tropical Fish Complete Pet Owner's Manual, Peter Stadelmann and Lee Finley (Barron's Educational Series, 2003)

Useful addresses

Most countries have organizations and societies that work to protect animals from cruelty and to help people learn how to care for the pets they live with properly.

UK
Royal Society for the Prevention of
　Cruelty to Animals (RSPCA)
Wilberforce Way
Southwater
Horsham
West Sussex
RH13 9RS
Tel: 0870 33 35 999
Fax: 0870 75 30 284

Australia
RSPCA Australia Inc
PO Box 265
Deakin West ACT 2600
Australia
Tel: 02 6282 8300
Fax: 02 6282 8311

Internet
UK
RSPCA
www.rspca.org.uk

There's a special kids' section as well as general information, message boards and links to shops at www.fishkeeping.co.uk

General fish keeping information at fish.orbust.net and www.thetropicaltank.co.uk

Message boards and discussion forum at www.fishforums.net

Australia
RSPCA
www.rspca.org.au

Disclaimer
All the Internet addresses (URLs) given in this book were valid at the time of going to press. However, due to the dynamic nature of the Internet, some addresses may have changed, or sites may have changed or ceased to exist since publication. While the author and Publishers regret any inconvenience this may cause readers, no responsibility for any such changes can be accepted by either the author or the Publishers.

Index

Titles in the *Keeping Pets* series include:

Hardback   0 431 12424 8

Hardback   0 431 12425 6

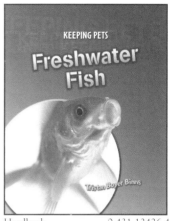

Hardback   0 431 12426 4

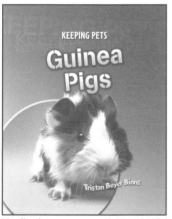

Hardback   0 431 12427 2

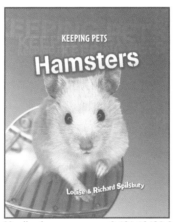

Hardback   0 431 12428 0

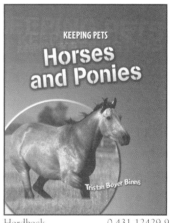

Hardback   0 431 12429 9

Hardback   0 431 12448 5

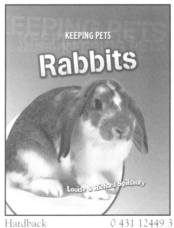

Hardback   0 431 12449 3

Find out about other titles from Heinemann Library on our website www.heinemann.co.uk/library